The Self Help Bible

Volume 2

How to Change the Life You Have

For the Life You Want

By Amanda Ball

Paperback edition first published in July 2011 through Lulu.com

ISBN 978-1-4478-1057-5

It is also available as an ebook through Lulu.com

Kindle version ASIN: B005GL94Y6

My Thanks

This book has, perhaps aptly, followed hot on the heels of my first volume of The Self Help Bible – About Self Esteem and How to be Confident.

I am grateful to my partner Julian, for his love and patience and for keeping our lives running while I spend time writing, as well as his help in editing. Also to my mentor Susan Beesley www.ChrisandSusanBeesley.com for her support and enthusiasm, not to mention her Internet Marketing expertise which she has shared so freely.

For my love of NLP and personal development I must thank Bruce Farrow of Helford 2000 www.helford2000.co.uk. Bruce is now one of the most qualified people in the NLP world, and the success of his business in a recession is testament to his amazing skill and dedication.

Finally I would like to thank you, the reader for making the choice to begin or continue your self development journey with my little book.

Enjoy! x

AJB 2011.

This book is dedicated to my sons,

Piers and Luca x

We begin to see, therefore, the importance of selecting our environment with the greatest of care, because environment is the mental feeding ground out of which the food that goes into our minds is extracted.

Napoleon Hill

Contents

Contents

Table of Exercises

What Are The Self Help Bible Books Based on?

If you have already read one of the other volumes of The Self Help Bible, then you will know that I am a Master Practitioner of NLP, Time Line Therapy™ and Hypnosis and studied psychology at university. I have worked as a manager, coach, therapist and counsellor and am a parent. I have drawn upon all these things to create this series.

Some of my coaching and therapy clients have allowed me to share their experiences with you, for which I am grateful. I have changed any information which might personally identify them.

I have structured the books quite deliberately and included exercises where possible, so that you can practice as you learn. Some of the material might be familiar to you and some may be new, you may well want to go back to certain bits and that's great.

Each volume will ultimately be available in an audio format, so that you can listen to it as well as read it. There are important benefits to this. Listening uses a different sense to reading, which helps the information to filter through to your unconscious and ensures that you have the tools you need, however you process information best, either by looking or listening.

I recommended that you do all the exercises for a minimum of 10 days. With focus and commitment, that's all it takes to start making real changes in your life; provided you consistently complete the exercise with energy and enthusiasm.

You'll know from the volume on communication if you've read it, that you wipe out most of what is going on around you, so you might find the same things covered in different ways. Again, this helps with the unconscious learning process.

Other things, which are new to you, will challenge your current thinking and feed another of your unconscious desires for new learning. Any time you contemplate something in a different way, you are expanding your horizons and breaking down preconceptions that you have created or accepted.

Just this one simple thing, the contemplation of something new or different, is enough to give you a new perspective and allow you to find the new, better choices available to you right now.

Where appropriate, you will find some (very simple) science. We are fortunate in that studies which began in the 1990's, have really helped to validate much of the theory that NLP put forward in the 1970's.

Doctors are now able to take magnetic images of the brain which show neural pathways and electrical energy, which show visually what is going on in the brain when we think, feel, move etc

Whilst this doesn't necessarily change the processes we use, it does help us to understand why they work, adding credibility and scientific evidence, to that which we already know works.

Of course, the best proof of the pudding is the taste, and you may be surprised to find that once you begin asking yourself the right questions and creating better beliefs, that the great results you can create for yourself are proof enough.

So why not allow your mind to believe that any change you want is possible for you now, if you simply accept that it is possible and follow some simple guidelines?

Where you are in your life right now, is the result of your best thinking to date. Imagine how much better you could be in the future, if you removed some of the obstacles you have placed in your way without even realising it; if you cleared your path ahead and punched a wonderful new destination into your built in Sat Nav.

A brilliant future has always been possible for you, why not set yourself an easier course to achieve it now?

What's in This Volume?

This volume is all about creating the right mental environment for you to thrive in so that you can make the changes you need to in order to create the life you really want.

With simple and effective exercises to help you make the changes you need to, it covers;

- Why having the right mindset is key to achieving success in any area of your life

- Positive thinking – how to change the way you think and to think positively in a practical way (no fluffy kittens!)

- Why claiming responsibility for your life is so important

- How to get better control of your reactions and emotions

- How habits are formed and how to break them

- How to change the meaning of past events which have held you back

This book will help you make your mind work for you in a more productive way, improve your frame of mind and give you a more positive outlook for a happier life, where success, in every area of your life, can be easily achieved.

How to Get the Most From

The Self Help Bible

Read

The first and most obvious thing is to read them! Start with a title that appeals to you so that you are motivated. This always helps get better results and will give you a chance to see that you like the style of the books and find them easy to follow.

Write things down

If you come to a part which really sounds right to you, makes sense more than others, or gives you that feeling – you'll know it when you see it - write it down. It's a great idea to keep a journal, so that you can look back at it later and see your progress.

When you come to a section with questions, write down your answers. It helps clarify things in your mind when you have to think about them enough to write them down and stops your mind drifting.

Only thinking about something allows room for you to lose focus without ever really answering the question, so I'd always recommend writing down both the question and your answer.

Committing something to paper has the added benefit of creating a physical thing from your thoughts. If you know anything about the Law of Attraction, you will know that what you focus on and create energy about is ultimately what you will attract into your life.

As Buddha said "All that we are is the result of what we have thought."

Commit

When it comes to the exercises, make sure you follow the instructions carefully and put as much energy into them as you can. Tell yourself that the quality of your future depends on it – because it does! No half measures, no matter how silly it might seem.

Remember you have unconscious patterns (habits) which, although ultimately created for your good, may hold you back and actually sabotage your best efforts. Prevent them from doing so by playing full out every time. No hiding, no lying to yourself, no excuses. Make the time and do it properly!

The more effort you put in, the more benefit you will get out.

My Invitation to You!

Using techniques similar to some of those described in The Self Help Bible series, I have had the privilege of helping people to let go of serious traumas, discard phobias which left them paralysed with fear, or compulsions which threatened to destroy their lives, in a matter of minutes.

I have watched as people unearthed deeply rooted limiting beliefs, which have held them back for almost their entire lives and then transformed them into empowering new beliefs, geared towards success.

I have worked with some fantastic people, who had **the one thing necessary to change lives; the desire to do so.**

I appreciate how busy your life already is and that fitting this in will take some effort on your part, so I have done my best to break things down into manageable chunks for you and create a series of short books, rather than the bigger ones I originally planned.

These short books will help you to harness the power you possess in your own mind, root out the things which have held you back and find new ways to move forward. They will show you how to reclaim your life and reap the rewards that brings and to become the person you really want to be.

They will give you a starting point and explain, in very simple terms, the why and the how. They will show you how inevitable your success is, once you get your unconscious mind to work for you and towards the life that you want.

I hope you will be inspired to better yourself, to seize opportunities and to achieve your true potential.

You are every bit as remarkable, and deserve your success, as much as any other human being on this planet.

It is yours for the taking, with the right mindset, the right system and your willingness to take consistent, focused action.

Every journey begins with a single purposeful step and often the destination is not where we expected it to be. Why not let today be the day you take the first step to a brighter future, in which you are being, having and doing exactly what you want?

Enjoy your journey x

Who Can Benefit From The Self Help Bible?

You Will Benefit From These Books If...

1. You are interested in and ready to invest time on your own personal development

2. You feel some areas of your life could be improved

3. You want to learn to communicate or understand others better

4. You want more success in your life

5. You want better relationships

6. You want to be happier

7. You want to understand yourself better

8. You want to get rid of negative thoughts

9. You want to be able to help other people

10. You want to be a better parent or teacher

11. You feel like something is holding you back

12. You want to create a specific mindset

13. You want to feel better about yourself

14. You just want more!

Where to Begin

All too often we start out doing something new, to make changes to our life in one way or another and then after a bit of time, we lapse back into our old ways, declaring that that 'diet, quit smoking plan, exercise regime, confidence booster' etc didn't work.

What we fail to acknowledge, even to ourselves, is that we didn't follow it properly and gave up. There is a direct and indisputable link between the number of people who fail and those who give up. In order to get the most out of this book, you will need to make some promises to yourself.

If you really want to make lasting change and improvement in your life, then you are going to have to work at it a bit, get tough with yourself and hold yourself accountable.

Sometimes we let ourselves slide off the hook when things get uncomfortable, as we begin to see possible flaws in our own character or sometimes we remember things we'd rather forget and we are afraid, or don't know how to deal with them. Other times it's because it's just too much like hard work.

Then there are the times that we start out all fired up, with great intentions and our motivation wanes, because it takes too long and we begin to doubt that it's even possible. That's known as the law of diminishing intent and I believe everyone is susceptible to it at times.

Whatever excuses you have come up with or accepted from yourself in the past, I want you to make a conscious decision today, that this time will be different.

Buy yourself a notepad or journal for this journey and begin it by writing to yourself, that today is a new beginning for you and that from now on you are only going to expect, give and accept, the best of yourself. You have to do this in order to get what you really want.

Imagine each thing you learn is like a step on a stair case. The more stairs you climb, the better view you will have and the more clearly you will see the choices available to you. At the top of the staircase there is the door to your future, what lies beyond that door is up to you.

Why Your Mindset is So Important

Imagine that your mindset is like the beam of a headlight. As you travel along your road, this beam will light your way. If the beam is dim and narrow, your view, choices, direction and the speed that you can travel at will all be limited and you will be unaware of anything that is not directly in front of you.

If the beam is too wide and bright, you may find that whilst you are able to take in more of what's around you, your focus is impaired and your sense of direction muddled. You may find it difficult to choose between all the options now available to you and to find the best road ahead.

Getting the right mindset is the key to achieving the life you want in any area, be that your career, your personal relationships, or simply how you feel about yourself. The easiest way to ensure that your mindset is the best that it can be, is through personal development.

Personal development is simply rehearsing who you wish to be and once you have improved the way you feel about yourself and your life, and the way you behave and communicate with others, everyone around you will benefit.

I would urge you however, first and foremost, to do it for yourself. All too often we push ourselves so far down our own list of priorities, that there doesn't seem to be any time left for us. Or, we allow limiting beliefs about what we deserve, how much time and energy we are worth investing in and our own fallible sense of self importance, to hold us back.

Please, make a pact today, to set aside **just 15 minutes a day** for yourself. Plan what you will do in that time and then stick to it. If you can't do more than 15 minutes right now, that's fine, and if you can manage more than 15 minutes that's fantastic! Self development should be about pleasure not pressure. Make your commitment achievable and you will very soon find that you can do a bit more. It will become easy to spend time on yourself, as your beliefs about the value it brings evolve and you remember how great it feels to be at the top of your game and in control of your life.

You owe it to yourself to have the very best life that you can and to be the very best version of yourself that you can possibly be.

You will feel better for it and you will be a much better example to those who matter to you.

You deserve so much more than you already have and the great thing is that you really can have it all!

Forget those ideas that there isn't enough to go around or that you shouldn't want more. They are just ideas created to keep us content and quiet; to stop us from being too aspirational and asking too many questions. They help to keep control of our huge society, maintaining peace and order.

If the majority of people follow the 'rules'; get an education, then a job working for someone else and behave in an acceptable way, and if more importantly, they are happy with that, then large groups of people can live together peacefully.

There is an amount of method in this madness; but it isn't the only way. Nor is it right for everyone.

I'm not suggesting that you have to suddenly start behaving out of character, breaking rules, or quit your job, but you can, and I believe should, think about what is really right for you now.

Are you living the life you really want right now? If the highest power in the universe, whoever that might be for you, was to suddenly give you the chance to design your life, would you make any changes?

Would you want to feel better, have more money, more time, more friends, or better relationships with those who count? Or perhaps less worry, stress, conflict, sadness, demands on your time or time on your own?

If you would like something in your life to be different, then the changes have to start with you. You have to be the very best version of yourself that you can. Just like a musical instrument, the better tuned it is, the sweeter the music. Like a racing car, the more highly skilled the driver, the faster the race and the more likely you are to achieve victory.

I bet, without much effort you can think of an area of your life where you accept absolutely no compromise. Where only the best will do. I also bet for most people it's external to you and very probably for someone else!

Many of us will put ourselves way out of our comfort zone and go to great inconvenience for our jobs or our friends. Do you make as much effort for yourself as you do for others I wonder?

Most parents will make far more effort on something for their children than they do on something for themselves for example.

What if I told you, that constantly seeking ways to improve yourself and taking responsibility for your own life and happiness, could make a fundamental difference to their lives too? You'd want to do that for them wouldn't you? Isn't it better for them to learn without even realising it, from your triumphs, rather than your failures?

Why is it that we encourage people to 'learn from their own mistakes' rather than their successes? I sometimes think we just go about life back to front!

At work, we often give more of ourselves than is good for us. We work more hours than we're paid to and in many cases 'going the extra mile' is expected without question. You'll find it in many modern job descriptions and company mission statements if you look.

We compromise our lives out of work, to make sure that we're well thought of in work. We break our own rules to fit in with theirs, in the hope of securing the next carrot, be that promotion, a pay rise, a bonus or even just keeping a job.

I can tell you from hard learned experience, that no-one will thank you or remember you for working long hours or ignoring your conscience for 'the business.'

If you want to make a difference, at home or at work, start by making a positive difference to yourself. Then you are in a position to help other people do the same. Be an inspiration to others by being a shining example to them of what is possible if you know yourself. Motivate them by daring to make your own happiness and give them the confidence to do the same.

Not only will your job be a more proportionate part of your life, your work place will be a happier one and ultimately happy workers are what make any business a true success.

You often hear talk about a 'work-life balance' and devote time and energy trying to ensure that both parts get their fair share. It leads to stress, worry and feelings of guilt and under achievement.

Well, I have an answer to that! **Stop trying to make a work-life balance, there is no such thing, there is only life.** You only have one shot at making it great so concentrate on the stuff that really matters.

I have a favourite story, told to me by a friend's brother a long time ago. It's about a young lion who was approaching adulthood and as a rite of passage, was expected to hunt, kill and eat an elephant.

He was by nature a confident creature and knew that he could hunt and kill his target without too much problem. He was however worried that he wouldn't be able to eat a whole elephant and would therefore look silly in front of his friends and bring shame upon his pride.

As he was destined to become the leader of the pride eventually, it was particularly important to him that he should succeed.

A little mouse who lived nearby, came upon the lion pacing and could see from his furrowed brow and shallow breathing that he was worried. Although it was not the normal course of events for a mouse to address the king of the jungle, the mouse was clever and keen to be of service to such a powerful potential ally. Swallowing hard and taking his courage in both hands, he asked the lion what he was so worried about.

In his anguish, the lion did not even question this blatant disregard for his status and gladly confided in the little rodent.

The mouse was a caring and sympathetic character and listened intently as the lion explained his dilemma. It was not a problem he had, or was ever likely to encounter, but he understood the principles involved; pride and the fear of rejection by his peers; and the mouse decided to look for a way to help the lion.

He realised the lion might have trouble accepting advice from such a lowly creature, so he invented a story about another lion who had faced a similar situation and of course been successful.

The lion listened carefully and the wisdom of the mouse's words was not lost on him. Through his tale of a fellow, mighty and revered lion, the mouse suggested that the lion might overcome his problem of eating a whole elephant, by simple breaking the elephant into smaller pieces first.

The lion, buoyed up by this tale and now convinced of his own impending success, set out on his quest.

He soon managed to secure his prey and following the advice of the mouse, quickly accomplished all the tasks he'd been set.

The lion became very famous in his jungle and the head of a great pride.

The little mouse for his part, became a great friend and trusted confidante of the lion, which meant guaranteed protection for the rest of his life and respect from all the other animals. As in all good stories, they all lived happily ever after. Apart, I suppose, from the elephant!

Ever since I first heard that story, I've literally broken tasks down in my mind into 'bites of the elephant' and retold the story many times over to friends and my children. The story still makes me smile now!

So, if you feel like you've been treading water, and that now is the time to take charge of your life and begin to achieve the things that you really want, then you will find that this book is exactly what you need to get started now.

Remember that the vast majority of people don't even get this far, so you've already taken the most important first step towards a better future.

By investing in this book, you have sent the message to your unconscious mind, and the universe, that you know you are worth making an effort for and that you are ready to make changes. Give yourself credit for having made the decision to find something new.

How Long Does it Take to Change Your Life?

Do you know how long it takes to change your life? Well I'll tell you!

You change your life in an instant.

The moment that you make that decision, that you make that commitment to yourself, your life is changed. Obviously, it is up to you to follow through and make sure that you do the work and consistently apply what you learn, to ensure that the change is beneficial and lasting.

Think about it for a moment. **If you cannot expect the best of yourself, how can you hope to find success?**

If you cannot give the best of yourself to yourself, then how will you face yourself - let alone anyone else?

If you accept anything but the best from yourself, then you are effectively declaring that you consider yourself unworthy of even your own effort. How can you then have a good idea of your own worth and healthy self esteem?

It all begins and ends with you!

I have created these books for you, with the intention of making you think and more importantly to encourage you to make yourself answer. Only to yourself, but the most important questions of all are sometimes those that you ask yourself and decline to answer.

Praise Yourself, Celebrate Your Success!

Giving yourself credit and praising yourself is the first habit you need to get into, because praise tells your unconscious mind to do more of whatever it got praised for. Your unconscious mind is very like a child in some respects and it enjoys doing things that give you a good feeling.

The act of praising accelerates the learning process and helps create habits much faster. Remember that habits are just things we have done so often that they become automatic. We do them without having to consciously think about what to do and in what order. Put another way, if you praise yourself, you'll learn faster and get better at something quicker.

If repetition is the mother or all skills, then praise is the father. Repeat and praise to embed new behaviours quickly and easily. Remember, personal development is just practising who you wish to be and you will become that person faster if you praise yourself.

Think about a child learning to talk. They start with nonsense which even their parents can't understand, and they quickly realise that when they try to talk they get massive praise.

This stimulates their unconscious to do more of the same and so they continue trying, which elicits yet more praise and they keep going until they get it right. What a great cycle! I call it the Praise Cycle – original I know!

The Praise Cycle

As we get older, we typically get less praise from others and so we must praise ourselves. Get into the habit of recognising when you do something well with both words (said out loud if possible) and a gesture. It only needs to be a jubilant 'Yes!' so no excuse!

Pat yourself on the back, literally, or squeeze your fist as you acknowledge you've done well and enjoy the positive feelings that knowledge brings.

Why is it important to do that? Well, you are building a stronger neural pathway, or link, between the thing that you are doing and a good feeling or positive state. A neural pathway is like a short cut in your brain between two things. The more often you use the pathway, the faster and easier the route becomes.

As a human being, you are programmed to do things which make you feel good, it's all to do with chemical reactions in the brain, the release of endorphins. So if, when you achieve something and notice the nice feelings associated with that achievement, you 'do' something to mark that feeling, (squeeze your fist and say yes for example...) the positive feeling itself will become linked to the action that you do.

Each time you do this, you are strengthening the link and creating what is known as an anchor. An anchor is just a link between two things, so that when one happens it triggers the other.

Like a smell bringing back an old memory for example, or a song reminding you of a person, place or time. You hear the music and immediately see a picture in your mind, remember something and get a feeling about it. These are common anchors.

By squeezing your fist when you feel really happy, excited, motivated or any other really strong positive emotion, you are linking these two things – the feeling and the fist squeezing - and later on, when you need to feel great, squeezing your fist will bring back those feelings for you!

It's like having your own happy button!

The other key ingredient is a smile. Plaster the biggest smile on your face that you possibly can! Smiling causes certain muscles to contract which squeezes your brain and makes it release chemicals designed to make you feel good! Even in moments of darkness, if you smile you will feel better. It doesn't have to be a real smile either, it works the same.

Exercise 1

Make Your Own Happy Button!

1. Every day for 10 days, each time you are feeling in a positive frame of mind, or you see or hear something that you enjoy, squeeze your fist, smile and say yes.

2. Each day, find a quiet moment to recall two or three times in the past where you have felt really great. It might be a moment where you achieved something unexpected, saw something breath taking, heard someone say something lovely to or about you or anything else that caused you to feel good. A positive feeling might be love, motivation, excitement, exhilaration, anticipation or joy for example and the more all consuming the moment was the better.

3. Then, taking each memory separately, close your eyes and in your mind go right back to that time as though you were there again. Imagine being in your body and experiencing that same rush. Look around inside yourself and see what you saw, hear what you heard and allow those wonderful feelings to flood over you.

    If you really engage in this exercise you will feel the same as you did in the moment, because your unconscious mind is unable to distinguish between what is happening for real and what is only in your imagination.

Furthermore, because you have this event in your memory banks and the outcome is a positive one, your unconscious will be anticipating that and helping you along.

4.   Choose a piece of music that makes you feel great. Play it every day for 10 days and as you listen, jump and dance around like crazy. Again, as you feel great, squeeze your fist.

You can combine number 2 and 3 in this exercise if you want to and play the music as you recall your memories. In this way you link the song and the positive feelings in your neurology, like a chain in your unconscious.

My happy song is *I Gotta Feeling* by The Black Eyed Peas, which was playing as I smashed my hand through a wooden board at a motivational seminar this year. (There's a video of this on my web site www.theselfhelpbible.com) Every time I hear that record now I find myself grinning and feeling great without even realising!

Positive Thinking

We hear a lot about positive thinking and its benefits. It is undeniable that a positive outlook will make you feel happier in general and your results are likely to be better than if you are more pessimistic.

What is positive thinking all about though really and why does it have an aura of being 'way out' or 'pink and fluffy' associated with it?

I think a much better way to describe the habit of positive thinking is to call it **deliberate, constructive thinking**. It's not about thinking everything and everyone is great, that's not realistic or productive and it's not about turning a blind eye to the areas of your life that need work.

Positive thinking involves focus and attention. It's about knowing what you want and focusing on that rather than the lack of it. It's about noticing the positive benefits in the situations which present themselves to you and turning things around in your mind to enable you to do so. Positive thinking involves a desire to find a gain from everything in life and to learn and apply those learnings.

The most important factor of all to remember, is that when we think, we use words and the words we use create our emotions. When you speak, either out loud or inside your head, your unconscious mind is listening and it takes everything personally, whether you are referring to yourself or not. If you constantly pick fault with others or highlight the negative, then that's what your outlook will become. So, in short, choose the things that you think about and the words you use carefully. As a rule of thumb, if you wouldn't say those things about or to the person you love most in the world, then don't say them at all – even in your head.

Focus is another very important factor. In the same way that the spectrum of control over your life runs through a scale with, 'Cause' at one end and 'Effect' at the other, so the way you focus goes from moving toward one thing, to away from the opposite thing. There is a video on my web site which explains this, www.theselfhelpbible.com

For example, you may wish you had more money, were more wealthy. In thinking about this you may be motivated to either move towards wealth or away from poverty. Both will move you in a similar direction, but one will do so positively, pulling you towards your goal and the other will push you away from the thing you fear.

Desires are much like magnets in that they attract things like themselves, so by focusing and directing your energy towards the thing you want, you will feel increased momentum and motivation the closer you get. If you are focusing on moving away from the thing you don't want, you will feel an initial impulse and energy, but this will fade as you get further from your start point and you will lose momentum. As you start to slide back and re-approach the thing you are trying to avoid, in this case poverty, you will be propelled into, often short lived, action.

You can use this knowledge to help monitor your thought patterns and train yourself to think more positively. Listen in to the conversations you are having with yourself and with others. Do you focus on the things you have and want, or the things you don't have and don't want?

You might like to picture a coin in your head and when you catch yourself thinking about moving away from something or a lack, picture the coin flipping and ask yourself what would be on the other side? Instead of thinking that you wish you weren't so overweight, picture yourself at your ideal weight. Instead of thinking you're fed up not having enough of x, think how great it is to have so much of it and really focus on how great it will be to achieve that.

Positive thinking involves retraining yourself so that when you start to go down a particular train of thought, you catch yourself and pull yourself back into line. Don't waste time going down the 'if, but, maybe' ladder. By all means have sensible contingencies, but don't kid yourself you are just planning or preparing, if what you are really doing is imagining 101 unlikely and mood quashing possibilities.

Remember, your unconscious can't tell the difference between imagination and reality, so going through trauma in your head is as damaging as experiencing it for real. If you don't need to, don't!!

If you need help to make your thoughts more productive and remove more unhelpful influences, you can find it in volume 1 of this series, About Self Esteem and How to Be Confident. You can download a free preview at www.theselfhelpbible.com which includes a self esteem evaluation exercise.

Are You Ready to Take Back Control of Your Life?

So, the first question you need to answer is, who is in control of your life and are you ready to accept responsibility for it?

You are probably familiar with the scientific theory of cause and effect, that doing one thing causes an effect on another, and this holds true for our minds too.

Imagine if you will, a scale, at one end you have 'Cause' and at the other 'Effect'. At one extreme of this scale you will find someone who is totally empowered and living their life by design (At Cause), taking responsibility for themselves, their life and making decisions both consciously and deliberately.

At the other extreme (Effect) you'll find life's victims and they are usually unhappy, unfulfilled people, with a negative mindset, who feel unlucky and hard done by. They are allowing other people and things to dictate what's happening in their lives.

Of course, this is a very simplified explanation. It's a sliding scale, with Cause at one end and Effect at the other and you may be in different places for different areas of your life.

For example, an assertive business man or woman may be very submissive at home, or vice versa. Some people are really strong in some areas of their life and not in others. No two people are the same.

Mindset Martyrs live at the effect side of life too, but they are slightly different, in that they may be happy on the surface and even believe that they sacrifice their own desires and wishes, to do things for others.

In general they are actually fulfilling a need in themselves, to feel needed and useful at a deeply unconscious level. If you know one of these types of people then you will know that whilst they can be very caring and helpful, they also let you know how caring and helpful they are and what they have to sacrifice in order to be so.

When they choose to move towards the 'At Cause' end of the scale, to accept responsibility for their lives and allow themselves to be happy without feeling guilty, they inevitably discover that they are able to have both a fulfilling life, with freedom of choice, and to be of service to others. Usually with even more impact than they were previously.

A clear mind, that gives freely with unconscious alignment, is one of the most powerful and transformational tools on the planet.

So, again, the first question is,

Are you ready to accept responsibility for your life today?

Can you accept that where you are right now, is as a result of all the choices that you have made to date?

Can you draw a line in the sand and say to yourself,

'I accept that where I am today is a direct result of everything I have ever thought, said and done and I declare that from this point on, I will live my life happily, with the knowledge that I have the power to create the life that I truly desire'

You might not feel ready to do that yet and that's fine; if you do feel able to do that right now, then great - Good for you!

In either case, keep reading and you will discover, little by little, new ways of thinking and new techniques, to lead you towards a place of empowerment and acceptance.

The flip side of this coin, the yin to the yang, is that as well as accepting responsibility for your own life, you also have to allow others to take responsibility for theirs. This can be liberating for you both, although if you have assumed responsibility for another, handing it back may meet with initial resistance! In the same way that someone else can only take control of your life or decisions and 'make' you feel a certain way if you choose to let them, so you can only do it for them if they let you.

As most of this process happens at an entirely unconscious level, changing what until this point has been the 'norm' and a habitual pattern for you both, may be uncomfortable and difficult at first. The message here though has to be persevere. New habits can be formed very easily if you just keep at it, practice and praise.

What Accepting Responsibility Really Means

Is it About Blame and Guilt?

I imagine, judging by the reactions of people I have said this to in person, that you may well be thinking at this point 'but when such and such happened to me, that wasn't my fault' or 'I couldn't do anything about that' or 'S/he did that, not me' or variations on that theme, so let's just clarify it a little.

When I ask you if you are ready to accept responsibility for where you are, all I am saying is, at every moment in your life you have choices. Choices to do 'thing a' or 'thing b', choices to do something or nothing at all, chances to do what you want to, or to bend to the will of another.

Often there are no right or wrong answers, but there are always choices. Even choosing not to do or say anything is a choice.

So, the exact spot you are in at the moment, is the place you have arrived at because of all the choices you have made, both <u>conscious</u> and <u>unconscious</u> ones.

I am not talking about apportioning blame or guilt. This is not about looking at your past and deciding whose fault it was, when something didn't go as well as it could have.

We can all look back with the gift of hindsight and recognise choices that could have been better, see moments where we were 'led astray' by someone else and blame either ourselves or others for things that didn't work out. It's a great way to waste some precious time and about as useful as boiling your head!

What's done is done. You cannot change the past BUT you can change the way you feel about it and therefore the way it affects your future.

Even in moments where you feel, for one reason or another, that you have no choice −be that an emotional restriction, such as obligation or guilt, a practical one such as finance or geography, or any other permutation − you always have a choice about how you react and how you behave.

Even in moments where you feel that you have no choice −you always have a choice about how you react and how you behave.

It may be in some instances that this is the only thing that you can control, it can however be the most empowering; the knowledge that even in your darkest hour you retain control, you remain 'At Cause', can be the thing that makes the difference, if you are willing to embrace the concept.

No other person can make you feel anything unless you choose to. They may know how to appeal to your good nature or manipulate you into feeling a particular way, but only if you let them. You have the absolute power over your emotions, you may have forgotten that fact or never learnt it well enough to use it properly, but this is just part of the enormous power that you posses and can use if you choose to.

When will now be the right time to accept and believe you are where you are because of choices you have made I wonder?

Now that you can accept that, allow it to create space in your mind, freedom from old binds and to be an enlightenment to take forward with you.

We will look at ways to deal with issues in your past which might be painful or unpleasant later; this is just the first step.

The reason that it's significant is that in order to be truly fulfilled in life, you need to be in the driving seat.

This doesn't mean you have to suddenly become hard and selfish, or calculating or aloof, it doesn't mean you should suddenly get everything right and if you don't you've failed. It just means that you are prepared to take responsibility for who and where you are and where and whom you wish to be.

It has a lot to do with your perspective too and what you notice and what you don't. Thanks to the way our brain is made and its limited processing capacity, we each have a unique and valid perspective. You process about 7 out of the two million bits of information your brain receives every second, so there's a lot of room for interpretation. More on this in the volume on communication.

So, start by taking ownership of where you are and your choices, rather than letting someone else decide what's right for you.

Exercise 2

Test Your Perspective

This is a fun exercise to do to show you how little you pick out of what's around you, but you need someone else to do it with. I've used it in corporate training sessions, one to one coaching sessions, or for fun with kids and it never fails to surprise.

1. Pick two colours that are easy to spot in lots of places in the room you're in. Now tell the person or group to look around the room and spot as many things of one of the colours as they can. Give them plenty of time (like 30 seconds) to have a good look and memorise the objects.

2. Now tell them to close their eyes and run through their list in their mind.

3. Now tell them to keep their eyes shut and call out as many things as they can of the other colour that are in the room.

4. Watch their faces as they struggle to remember any! You'll probably get a few answers but it will be hard.

5. Then ask them to reel off the list of the things of the other colour that they memorised and you'll see how much easier it is.

What this demonstrates in a fun way, is that although you were all in the same place, looking at exactly the same things, you will have noticed and remembered different things. Some people will spot tiny details and get a long list, others will only notice the really obvious ones and swear there aren't any more. It's just different filters and perceptions that's all and the way we make our picture of the world and our life works in exactly the same way.

When you allow someone else to decide for you, whether their decision turns out well or not, it will never be as great as if you make the choice for yourself. When it works out well, you'll be pleased, but there will always be that part of you that knows that they made the decision and therefore the great result is not entirely down to you. If the outcome is less favourable, whilst you might find some consolation in the fact that it was their decision, you will still hear that little voice telling you that you should have chosen for yourself and whilst you can apportion blame to them, you are likely to feel some yourself and probably a bit of guilt too.

Imagine instead, that you decide. It might not turn out to be the best decision, but it will mean that you are empowering yourself, declaring yourself capable of deciding to take responsibility for yourself. Look at the result, work out what might have been better and therefore what you can learn to apply next time. Don't blame yourself or feel guilty, instead feel proud that you made a choice and know that you now have extra knowledge for the future.

Even better then, when you make a choice that works out well for you, you can really rejoice! You already have a great result AND you get to keep all the credit for yourself. By all means seek opinions from others if it helps you to make your decision – remember it's better to learn from others mistakes than to make your own! But keep it in perspective, their opinion is only their opinion, not the only, or necessarily the right, answer.

Exercise 3

Positive Replay

1. Think of a time in the past, where you have let someone else decide on a course of action, where the outcome was not ideal.
   a. What could you have done instead?
   b. What could you have learnt from that time?
   c. Did you repeat the mistake?

2. What would you like to do differently next time?

3. What's stopping you?

4. Imagine a similar situation occurring in the future and that this time you choose what to do, which results in a great outcome.
   a. What will you need to do in order to get that outcome?
   b. What will you not be able to do?
   c. How will you know you've been successful?
   d. How will that feel?

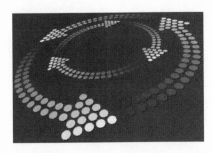

Choose Your Response

At this point I expect you might be thinking, 'Sometimes you can't choose; some things are out of your control' and of course I'd have to agree with you. There will always be parts of your life over which you have <u>less</u> decision making power.

Anything that involves the free will of another for example, or is subject to a set of rules or regulations will restrict your choice, not to mention death and taxes, BUT, here is the really cool thing and the essential point of this chapter.

Even when you do not have total control of a decision, you always get to choose how you deal with and react to the situation.

Now you might well be thinking, as I used to, 'that's all very well, but sometimes you just can't help the way you feel.'

Wouldn't it be cool then if I could give you some tools which would help you be more aware of and regain control of your emotional state.

The first step to change is awareness, you have to start to notice the things you haven't noticed until now. I would like to share with you a tool I developed a few months ago to help a client who found it difficult to control his moods and who found he was often reacting inappropriately to situations, or being overcome by negative emotions. It is like a three step check to assess your reaction quickly and I call it the RAG test. We'll look at some scenarios after the exercise.

When talking about negative emotions, I am typically referring to the big 5, **Anger, Sadness, Fear, Hurt and Guilt**. I think that any other negative moods, frames of minds and emotions fall under one of these. If you feel that for you, there is another negative emotion that doesn't fit under one of the 5, that's fine, there are no right or wrong answers and your interpretation is every bit as valid as mine ☺

Exercise 4

The R.A.G Test

Here are 3 really simple questions that you can ask yourself, or someone else, when you spot a negative reaction, mindset or behaviour pattern. They only need a yes or no answer to start with, so you can use this test anywhere at any time.

1. Is it **Reasonable**?

    Is it reasonable or understandable that you are reacting to this thing at all? If you were trying to explain this to someone else, and telling them what had happened, would it be clear to them why you had reacted? Would it make sense that you felt some kind of emotional response?

2. Is it **Appropriate**?

    Is your reaction appropriate given the situation and is it proportionate? This is for you to decide based on your own values, attitudes and beliefs. Remember that your opinion may differ from someone else's.

3. Is it **Good** for you?

    This is the key one. Is the response you are currently having, or the behaviour you are 'doing' good for you? Is it the best response for you, or is there something else you could do which would serve you better?

Now, the deal is this. If you can answer yes to all 3 questions, then you don't need to change anything. BUT if you answer No to any of the questions, then you need to stop what you are doing and do something differently.

The great thing about this is, that by the time you have asked and answered the questions (number 2 seems to cause the most debate!) you have already broken into the pattern and shifted your focus. This then leaves the way clear for you to decide what to do about it.

Often, simply thinking about the trigger, the thing that caused your reaction, can be enough to take the sting out of the tail and lighten your mood. You may find it easy to quickly resolve how you feel about what triggered your reaction.

Let's look at some examples of how this might work.

Scenario 1

You are out driving when someone cuts you up or pulls out in front of you dangerously. You react very angrily, blasting the horn, shouting and gesticulating. Not an uncommon occurrence, but,

1. Is it **Reasonable**?
2. Is it **Appropriate**?
3. Is it **Good** for you?

Of course this is subjective and you may argue either way for 1 and 2, but 3 has to be a resounding no. You are probably feeling anger, at the very least your blood pressure is raised, your heart racing and your concentration impaired. How is any of that good for you?

In order to move on from the experience and change your mood, you can just invent a story to go with it. Imagine that the person has just had a call from the hospital and someone they love is ill. Now do you still feel angry? For all you know, that may be the case and it doesn't matter. What matters is that you feel better and regain control of your emotional state. My favourite is to say out loud 'thank you for reminding me how important it is to be a considerate driver!' Interpret that how you will!!

Scenario 2

You are reading a tragic story in the paper and find yourself crying and imagining how awful it must feel to be in the situation of the person in the story. You are being sympathetic and even empathetic but;

1.   Is it **Reasonable**?
2.   Is it **Appropriate**?
3.   Is it **Good** for you?

Again, you decide on question 1 and 2 but number 3 has to be a no. Apart from making you feel miserable, it has been shown that this kind of mood lowers your immune system making you more susceptible to illness. By imagining yourself in that kind of situation you are focusing on the negative and therefore attracting negativity. Even if you are thinking that you are fortunate not to be in that position, you are still focusing on and thinking about that undesirable situation.

I think that we often get caught up in the illusion that in order to be 'nice' people, we have to share the pain of other people and the media thrives on our desire to do so. Sharing pain doesn't actually help anyone, particularly anonymously.

Start by avoiding unnecessary negative emotions of any sort for yourself and then help others to do the same, that has got to be a better way to live for all concerned. It doesn't mean you don't care, it just means you keep yourself in a better position to be of real help.

Rather than helping suffering, alleviate pain.

If you then need help to change your frame of mind once you have decided it is not the best choice available, you can either refer to Volume 1 of this series and an exercise called 'STOP', or prepare in advance some positive memories you enjoy thinking about instead, or use your happy button, if you've already made one. Change your posture and your breathing if you can, to help change your mood.

Scenario 3

Just to prove that I haven't rigged the test, now imagine that you are out walking when you are confronted by a ferocious bear. Filled with fear, you shout and turn and run, empathetic but;

1. Is it **Reasonable**?
2. Is it **Appropriate**?
3. Is it **Good** for you?

This time it's a resounding yes to all three, so just keep on running!

Change Your Perspective

If you ever get frustrated by your own reaction to things and wish you could behave in a different way automatically that would serve you better, start by working out what you would rather be doing instead. Then, make yourself do that new thing instead and praise yourself each time you do it.

To begin with it might feel false and contrived and that's quite normal, because you are behaving or reacting very consciously. In other words, your behaviour is deliberate rather than automatic. Persevere though and in no time at all, you won't have to think about doing it any more, it will just happen and, because you have praised the action, you'll feel good about it too!

What we perceive to be real is only 1 possible interpretation of the information available to us. There's a volume of The Self Help Bible dedicated to communication which explains this in more detail.

When we make our invisible world in our heads out of the things we sense through our 5 senses, (taste, touch, sight, smell, hearing) we are effectively framing the situation to support our current beliefs, values and attitudes and choosing to pay attention only to the bits that fit.

If you imagine a painting, you can see that how the overall image looks will be greatly affected by the frame around the picture. So why not learn to do this with your mind?

What reframing does is to offer you the chance to examine things in a different context. It's a bit like looking for the silver lining in the cloud.

Changing the frame changes the meaning or the context and therefore gives you the choice to react and behave in a different way too.

An easy way to explain this, is to imagine that your problem is a box and you are inside the box. From here, all you can see are the walls of the problem and your viewpoint is very limited.

Once you can step outside of the problem, (the box) you can see it from all sides and angles. You can move closer or further away to get different vantage points and ask other people for their opinion and help. You can see the problem more objectively and proportionately and begin to see its possibilities rather than just its limitations. Perhaps this is where the phrase 'Think outside the box' comes from?

Exercise 5

Change Your Perspective

Changing the way you view and feel about something can be hugely beneficial to you and can drastically improve your whole outlook

You can do it really easily too. As ever, awareness is the first key to change, so your acceptance that this is only one interpretation of the information available is a brilliant first step. Then start by asking yourself a question which would alter the meaning.

Think of a situation, behaviour or challenge that you dislike or that makes you feel negative in some way and ask these questions

> **1.** What is a different way to see that?
> **2.** What else could that mean?
> **3.** What else could I hear in that message?

Already, just by asking yourself these questions, you are acknowledging that there is another way to interpret the 'facts' and you are interrupting your thought process and allowing room for manoeuvre, by challenging what you would have previously accepted without question. Did you feel that stretch? That was your comfort zone expanding to take in this new theory!

Of course you must make sure that the new frame you create is a positive one for it to be beneficial and even if it feels a bit false, saying the words creates a better emotion which can only be to your benefit!

You can try thinking about having the same reaction in a different context, how would that change the meaning? For example, if someone was trying to mislead you and you refused to back down, your behaviour might be labelled as 'assertive' or 'tenacious'. The same behaviour in a different context might be deemed 'stubborn' or 'obstinate'.

In this example, it's the context which has changed or been reframed.

Try the 'as if' frame. This time you can imagine dealing with the situation 'as if' you have the resources you need. You can do this in a number of ways:

- Imagine that you are someone else who knows exactly what to do. What would they do to resolve the situation?
- Imagine that you are looking back from the future, once the problem has been solved and ask yourself how you came to solve the problem.
- Imagine you had a magic lamp with a genie in it, who could change one part of the situation you're struggling with. How would that affect things?
- Imagine you already know all you need to know to solve the problem. What is it that you hadn't realised you knew, that will change the circumstances now?

In all cases you are changing your perspective and that is the key to beginning to solve your problem.

Whilst you can never be 100% sure of someone else's motivation, reframing a situation involving someone else can be extremely beneficial. If you are faced with someone who refuses to accept the possibility of an alternative opinion to their own (we all know at least one of those!) or if someone is struggling to find another way to see something, there are some great questions you can use. Even if they are unable to answer them, you asking the questions will start a process in their brain which will make them <u>consider</u> what you have asked. They have to imagine what you've said even to discount it. Just as if I say to you, 'don't think about a blue dog barking' you will make a picture of it in your mind. This alone will signal to their unconscious that there is another alternative and one of the strengths of the unconscious is filling in gaps and finding links and patterns between things.

I will use an example to illustrate the point, imagine someone is saying

> *"I can't take control of my life because I don't feel confident enough."*

Here are 10 things you might say in response to that, each one relates to a different NLP language pattern, but you don't need to know the detail of that for it to work. It's sufficient to understand that each time you are challenging or changing a particular aspect of that belief, which signals that it is not a cast iron fact. Remember that the beliefs we hold are only things we have chosen to accept as true, usually unconsciously and often very early in life. They are changeable and very fallible.

1. *When you were little you didn't know how to write but you can do that now can't you?*
2. *How well are you controlling that belief?*

3. *What would happen if you did feel confident enough / take control?*
4. *What's stopping you?*
5. *How do you know that's true as you sit here right now?*
6. *Which bits of your life do you feel you can't control?* Make them specific, all of it is not an answer! Ask, *what specifically?*
7. *It's not about your confidence or ability to take control, it's about how soon you can notice all the areas of your life that you already control beautifully*
8. *Maybe it's not that you can't control your life, maybe it's just that you are moving out of your comfort zone as you begin to control it?*
9. *Have you ever been successful at something even though you didn't feel confident to start with?*
10. *Isn't that like saying you can't drive a car before you start driving lessons?*

Think back to a disagreement you might have had with someone. Would your behaviour or theirs have been appropriate in a different set of circumstances? If so, then that would imply there is a learning that you can take from it and some feedback to be found (remember, one of the first principles of NLP is there's no failure, only feedback!)

I truly believe that if you can learn something from a situation, then no matter what that situation was, it was not pointless and you can gain from in.

There is a lovely Taoist story which illustrates the concept of reframing beautifully.

An old farmer was envied by his neighbours because he was wealthy enough to own a horse. One day the horse ran away. The neighbours lamented for the man and his loss. The farmer simply said "Why do you assume this is a bad thing?" and went about his business.

Sometime later the horse returned, bringing with it two beautiful wild horses. The neighbours were jealous but the man simply said "Why do you assume this is a good thing?" and went about his business.

His only son tried to ride one of the horses and was thrown, breaking his leg in the process. The man's neighbours were sorry for the man but he simply said "Why do you assume this is a bad thing?" and went about his business.

A few days later, war broke out and all the young men were conscripted to the army with most never returning, apart from the man's son who was not drafted because of his broken leg.

How Patterns and Habits are Created

If I had to sum it up in one word, repetition!

Your unconscious mind is constantly trying to find familiarity, in order to make sense of the world for your conscious mind and to support your beliefs.

As you go through life experiencing things, it's continuously checking in on you and comparing with its own filing system, to see if you've had a similar experience before.

If you have, it finds a match and will use the information stored to decide how to proceed. You will probably feel like you did the last time, or like you have most often, in this kind of situation.

If the outcome of the situation then turns out to be the same, this will compound the encoding of this type of experience and the next time you encounter a similar situation, the association will be even stronger.

What this means is that as you come up against a situation, you will automatically feel and expect things to go a certain way. If things then turn out like you thought they would, this will make the feeling even more certain and powerful the next time.

You are creating unconscious patterns and developing habits and it now becomes very apparent how phobias and fears develop doesn't it?

Imagine, you see a spider as a child and as you see it the grown up next to you starts screaming. Without understanding why, and because you trust adults, you will believe that a spider is something to be afraid of and you will experience a feeling of fear, even if at that stage you can't articulate it as such.

The next time you see a spider your unconscious mind will recall the previous time and the emotion associated with it, FEAR. You will automatically feel afraid, even if only a little bit to start with.

If you again experience something negative, say it crawls on you, or someone else shows fear, your negative association with spiders will be reinforced and made even stronger.

So, the next time you see one, your unconscious now has more and more previous history on which to base its reaction and the reaction will become stronger as a result.

These associations can become so strong that they can be triggered merely by a thought or a word. Moreover, the time between you becoming unconsciously aware of the trigger and your response to it, is so short that you may even start to react before you actually see (assuming the trigger is visual) the thing you are afraid of.

Ask someone who is afraid to fly, to close their eyes and imagine being on a plane and just watch what happens. They are not suddenly put on a plane, so there is no physical cause for their reaction, but they will experience very real emotions and sensations none the less.

This is the unconscious at work, setting in motion the chain of feelings and accompanying symptoms that it has come to link to flying.

It's a bit like making a string of pearls. Each similar experience puts another pearl on the string and so the string gets longer and stronger with each experience.

NLP and Time Line Therapy™ use specially developed techniques to remove the first pearl on the string, so that all the others just fall away. This clears the way for you to start a whole new pattern of doing something, whatever it might be, and creating more beneficial habits.

If you find that you 'usually' react in a particular way in certain circumstances, as we have already seen, the first key to changing that is to have an awareness of the pattern. Once you have identified it you can move on to thinking about what you would like to do instead and then it's simply a case of practising.

Exercise 6

Change Your Reaction

Take a piece of paper with three columns headed, "When" "I Used to" and "Now I."

When	I used to	Now I

Think about your automatic behaviour in certain situations, what you do out of habit, that when you think about it later, you wish you could do differently. The things that make you frustrated at yourself or feel negative in some way.

Example 1

Sue is a bit shy. If she is in a situation with people she has only met once or twice before, she always assumes they won't remember her and feels that she'll look stupid if she tries to talk to them. She tries to avoid the situation and because of this people often describe her as snooty or aloof. She wishes she could find the courage to just go and talk to them.

Her form might look like this:

When	I used to	Now I
I see people I don't know very well	Pretend I hadn't seen them or look away	I smile and go and talk to them, remind them of where we met if I need to, and still feel good

In the first column, she describes the situation or set of circumstances which can lead to the type of behaviour she would like to change.

In the second column, she describes the behaviour itself, what she would currently do.

In the third column she will write down how she wishes she could react instead. It's important to have the outcome at the end, how she will feel and any other positive benefits this new behaviour will bring, because that's the motivator.

Example 2

Phil finds it hard to accept criticism and when his boss gives him feedback at work he gets very defensive and reacts badly. His entry might read:

When	I used to	Now I
My boss gives me feedback on a piece of work	Feel frustrated and upset and act sulky	Listen. Thank him for his feedback, think about what he's said and how I can use it to improve next time. Feel good that he has taken the time to consider my work and feel great at my new reaction!

Write a few of these each day until you have a good list and read them through (preferably out loud) once a day. Here's why this is such a useful exercise.

You are clearly telling your unconscious that there is another way to react in these situations, that will have a more positive benefit for you. Your current behaviour is described as being in the past already, which clears the way for the new behaviour to root itself firmly in your unconscious. Imagine that time itself is stretched out in a long line and that you can only look at one thing at a time. By framing the current behaviour in the past, you are mentally pushing beyond the boundaries of that habit, pushing into the place where you store past experiences and memories, so that there is room in the now for a new way of reacting. It's like putting down a big, dusty old box so that you can hold a big shiny present instead!

Describing your new reaction as though you already behave that way, moves your perspective and clears the way for the new behaviour.

By ending the new behaviour with a statement about how you now feel, you are creating a positive frame for the situation and setting yourself up to feel good. Your unconscious likes familiarity, so by telling it how you're going to feel when you do react in the new way, when you get there, you are most likely to feel exactly as you've described, which compounds and accelerates the process.

Next of course comes the practical element and once you have created some really compelling outcomes in your third column and read them through a few times, you will be eager to try them out! Find opportunities in your daily life to try out your new behaviours. When you spot a situation you have described on your list, adapt your reaction to match column three on the list. Then, celebrate your victory over that old way of reacting and praise yourself for taking charge of your life one step at a time.

You might find it helpful to pick two or three behaviours to work on first, then once you've mastered them, move on to some others.

At first it will be a very controlled and conscious reaction, but, remember, only you know that! Other people might spot something is different when you react in a way they are not expecting, but this will largely be at an unconscious level and do you know what – who cares! This is all about you!!

Each time you 'do' this new behaviour, it will become a little more automatic, until it becomes your automatic response in that kind of situation. Praising yourself each time will help accelerate the process and, once you get used to doing it, it feels good to acknowledge something you've done well.

The Competence Cycle

The 4 Stages of Learning

You may already have heard of, or be familiar with the Competence Cycle, even if you haven't known it to be labelled as such.

It very simply shows you the four stages you go through when learning to do something new, from the start point where you aren't even aware that you don't know how to do something, to where you are able to do it without thinking about it. By the time you get to the third stage, the task is well within your comfort zone.

An interesting thing, is that this cycle applies to both intentional and unintentional learning. So, things like phobias, habits and compulsive behaviours follow exactly the same pattern. Because you have learnt to do them so well that you can do them without thinking, they feel like a natural response now, but actually they are just a response that you have repeated and mastered over time.

Great news though, as it clearly shows yet again that you can learn a different way to react!

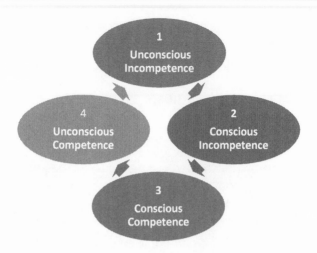

The 4 Stages of the Competence Cycle

1   Unconscious Incompetence

You don't know how to do it

You don't see the benefit in doing it

You don't want to do it

You don't know you don't know how!

2   Conscious Incompetence

You don't know how to do it

You realise the benefit in doing it

You know you don't know how!

3   Conscious Competence

You know how to do it but you still have to think about how to do it

You have to concentrate whilst doing it

You are doing it consciously

You know you know how!

4   Unconscious Competence

You can do it without thinking

You do it unconsciously

Another important point with learning is that being a cyclical process, you can slip from position 4, back to position 1. In other words, you can do something so unconsciously that you actually lose the ability to do it well.

A great example of this is driving. Do you think that if you were asked to resit your driving test now that you would pass? The chances are that you would not! That is not to say that you don't drive well anymore, simply that you will have developed habits that you did not have, when you first learned to drive and took your test and that would mean you now don't drive in the required text book fashion.

Change How You Feel About the Past

Tell a Different Story

Stories are a wonderful vehicle for conveying messages to the unconscious mind. You only have to think back to the stories you heard as child to see that many of them will have had a hidden message, or a moral. Even when we are grown up, our mind still loves to root out what's left unsaid or written between the lines.

If you want to get a message through to children, stories are the perfect medium. The less obvious it is the better, but your tales don't have to be sophisticated.

If you have to deliver presentations or training courses, a story is a great way to begin. I have told stories to board members before and although they might be surprised, provided they are a proportionate part of the session, relevant and well told, they always get a good reception. There are some great books available on metaphors for trainers, so you don't even have to make them up.

One thing we are usually unaware of, is that we are constantly telling ourselves stories and then we accept them as infallible truths, construct limiting beliefs from them and often keep them forever.

Did you ever have a nickname as a child that still pains you to think about today? Have you ever met someone thin who still regards themselves as fat, despite the obvious evidence they see daily?

These are just two examples of where we make a story for ourselves. The good news is that you can change these stories, as easily as you can a fairy tale, with a simple technique.

Furthermore, if you wish to, you can actually change the way you feel about any event in your past. You cannot change the past, but you can change the emotion associated with it. This alters the way you feel in the present and will change your behaviour and results in the future.

We have all seen, done or experienced something in our past that will have caused us to feel bad in some way; less than someone else, wrong, worthless, guilty, sad, the list is endless and in each case this will have caused you to have questioned your self worth. Given that your self worth contributes to your self esteem and that a healthy level of self esteem is the foundation of any positive mindset, you can see now how important this is.

Hopefully, by the time you reach this point in the book you will have begun to see that your perspective on any situation is only one way to see it. Your description is only one way to describe with words what you are feeling inside and like everything that goes on in your mind, it is bound by your grasp of language and your understanding of the world and the situation at the time of the event.

So, going back to the time you were teased as a child, or even worse bullied, or given any label at all, how great was your understanding of the world at that time? Was the way you reacted the only possible reaction available to you then or now?

Exercise – 7

Change the Story

1. Create a list of events in the past, that caused you to doubt yourself in any way or to feel bad. Don't go into a lot of detail, but give each story or event a title that you will understand. This might be something you were aware of at the time it happened, or the root cause of something that you have since recognised.

2. Now to change the meaning of the story. Firstly, given the perspective and enhanced understanding that you now have, the power of hindsight and the lack of emotion for the situation, think about another possible meaning for the story that makes it less painful than it was before. Write it down,

3. Once you have done this, think of another possible meaning, this time a positive and empowering one and write it down.

4. Rewrite your story with the new meaning.

5. Stand up, shake yourself out and then read it to yourself. Take deep breaths and close your eyes and rewatch the scene as it would have happened with your new meaning. Picture it as though you are there, in your own body, looking through your own eyes. Look around you so that you can see what you would have seen, hear what you would have heard and felt the wonderful, empowering feelings this new story would have given you.

Take as long as you like to enjoy the feelings and as you do so, squeeze your fist.

When you are ready to come back to the present, open your eyes, and then give yourself a big dose of praise.

Confirm to yourself, that for ever more, that story will stay as you just left it and thinking of it will only serve to make you feel fantastic!

6.   As you go forward, notice, acknowledge and celebrate new situations where, if they had happened in the past, you would have reacted in that old way, with those old negative emotions. Notice how you now react differently, in an empowering and positive way, now that your story has changed and you have broken the chains that bound you before.

Here's an example from one of my clients, Kim. Kim had, for as long as she could remember, hated her teeth. To anyone else they looked fine but when she pictured herself she saw teeth like a horse and did her best to keep them concealed. She hated speaking in public because of this and was shy and introverted.

When we explored this, Kim discovered that this all stemmed from a nickname given her by her father when she was about 11 when her first adult teeth came through, Tombstone Lil.

Kim had, at the age of 11, heard this teasing and created her story that she had abnormally large and ugly teeth. Once she had grown a bit, her teeth were perfectly proportionate and the nickname died but Kim never changed her story.

By changing her story to a different meaning – that her teeth were noticeably nice and that her Dad loved to tease her because he knew she'd take it in good part – she changed completely the way she felt about herself. She was much more confident and able to engage with others more easily as a result. She couldn't react in the same way she had before, because the root cause of her problem no longer existed. It's like taking the main ingredient out of a recipe; you just can't make the same dish anymore.

Changing the story doesn't change the past, but it does allow it to become more positive and helpful for the future. Why would you choose anything less?

About The Author

Amanda Ball

I am a very proud mum and a Master Practitioner of NLP, Time Line Therapy™ and Hypnosis. Helping other people to realise their potential, has been a love of mine for many years. It started as a sideline, then, fed up with the constant grind of the corporate world, I gave up my well paid job in order to pursue this passion.

A year or two on and having tried lots of different things, I am now concentrating on writing and coaching/counselling which I love.

www.JulianandAmanda.com is the home of the business that I now run with my partner Julian.

We understand that the most successful people in all walks of life, whether that be in business, sport or relationships, all first devoted time to their own self development. We now successfully provide coaching and mentoring, in the personal development field, to a growing number of people. We specialise in helping them get their head in the right place, to take their life and business where they really want to go.

We also provide an online library of personal development resources, which is available to everyone. Please feel free to take a look and see if there is anything else which may be of value to you. Why not bookmark our page, or take the RSS feed, to be automatically updated whenever we add something?

....And Lastly

I really hope that you found this book interesting and thought provoking and I hope that you will invest the time in yourself to use the techniques included. I know that if you do, you will really make a positive difference to your own life and to those who are influenced by you.

This book is the one of a series and for more information on the other titles go to http://theselfhelpbible.com

You might like to join me on Facebook at http://facebook.com/theselfhelpbible or follow me on Twitter @selfhelpbible

I am always interested to hear about your views, so please email me at the address below with your comments and feedback and if you've enjoyed the book, please post a review at Lulu.com or on Amazon.

Thanks for reading and have a great day!

Amanda

Email Amanda: amanda@theselfhelpbible.com

16956924R00044

Made in the USA
Lexington, KY
19 August 2012